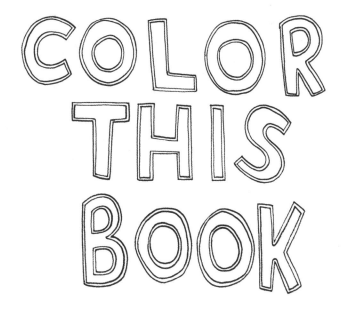

COLOR THIS BOOK

NEW YORK CITY

BY ABBI JACOBSON

CHRONICLE BOOKS

SAN FRANCISCO

Statue of Liberty

Street Vendors

The High Line

New York Public Library Main Branch, Midtown

Grand Central Terminal

Times Square

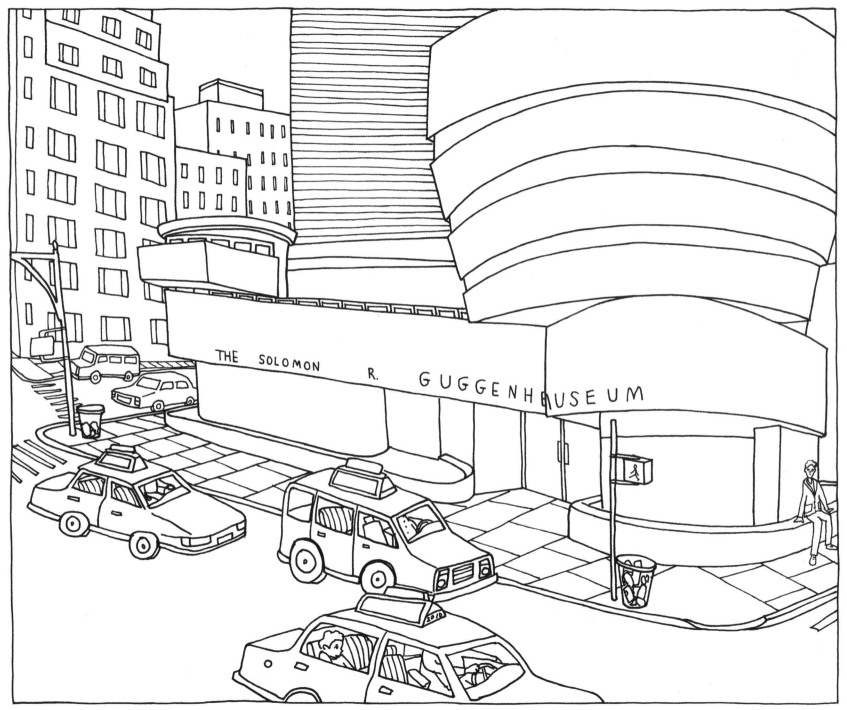

Solomon R. Guggenheim Museum, Upper East Side

Mamoun's Falafel and Caffe Reggio, Greenwich Village

Artichoke Pizza, Greenwich Village

A NYC Subway Platform

Bethesda Fountain, Central Park

Subway Drummers

Union Square Greenmarket, Union Square

Strand Bookstore, East Village

Broadway Theatre District

The City Bakery, Flatiron District

Katz's Delicatessen, Lower East Side

Charging Bull Statue, Wall Street

The Spotted Pig, West Village

Brooklyn Bridge

Washington Square Park

Gay Street, West Village

Upright Citizen's Brigade Theatre, Chelsea

Chinatown

Flatiron Building, Flatiron District

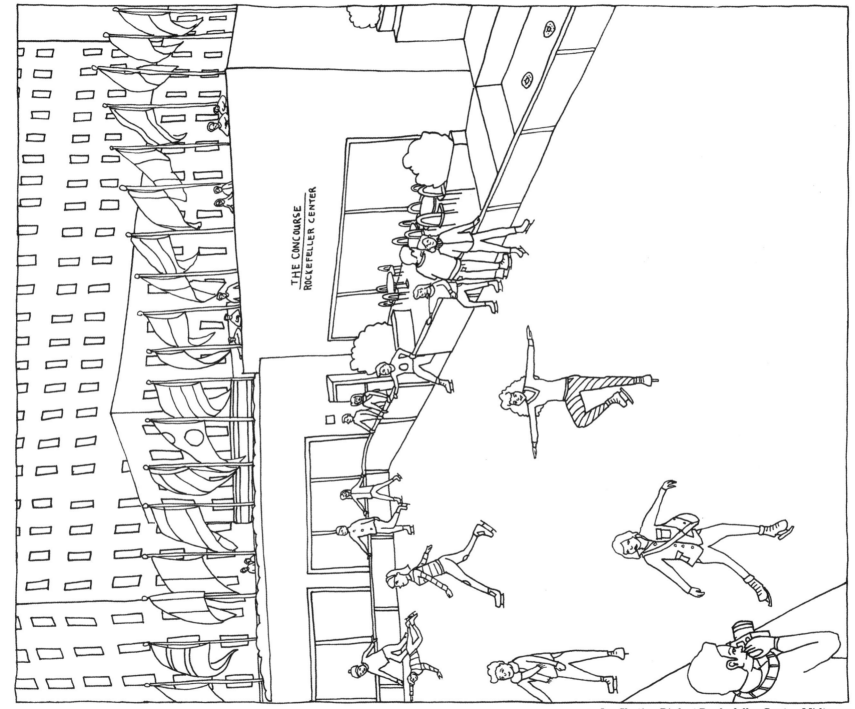

THE CONCOURSE
ROCKEFELLER CENTER

Ice Skating Rink at Rockefeller Center, Midtown

Tribeca